AF225800

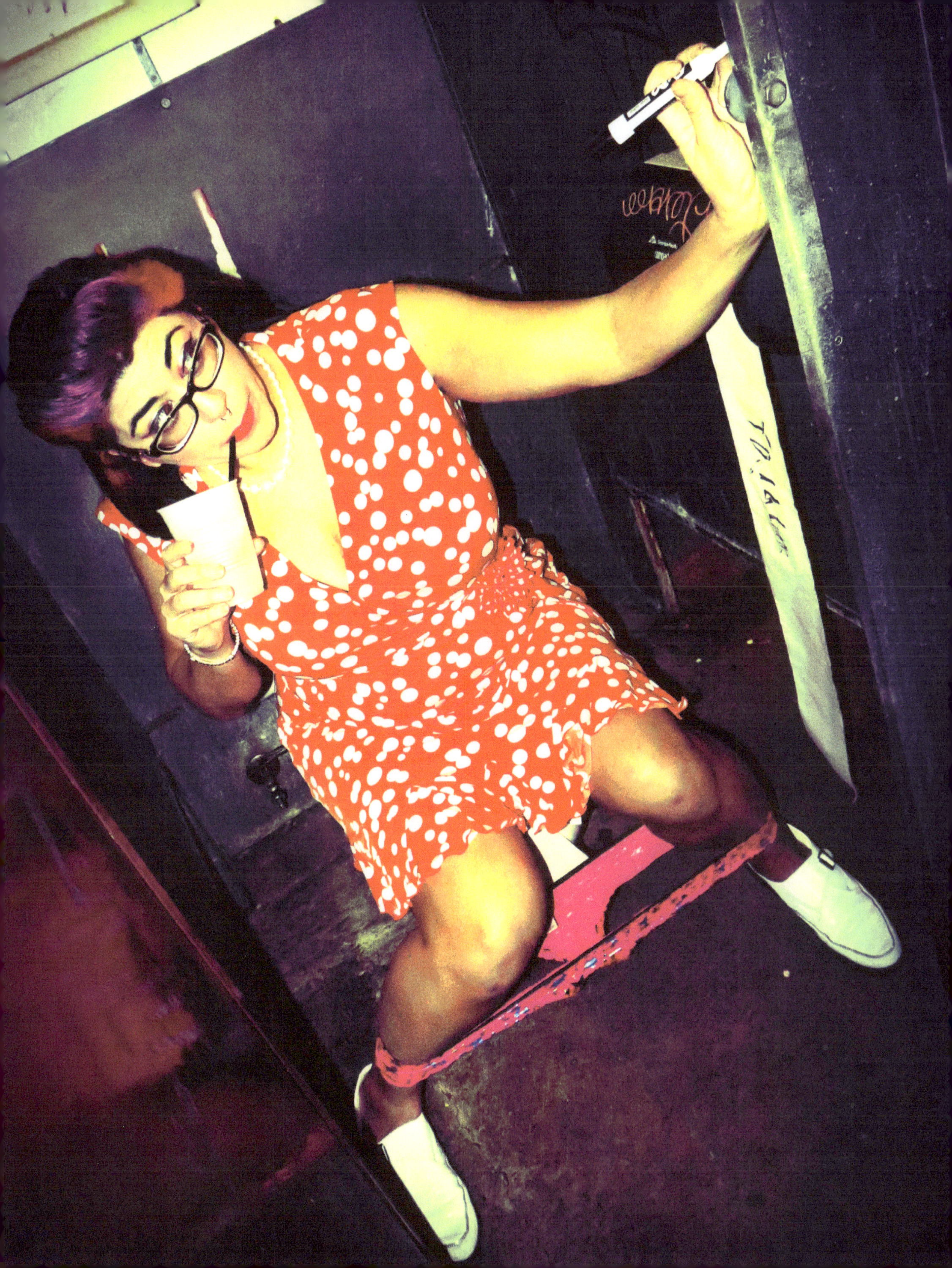

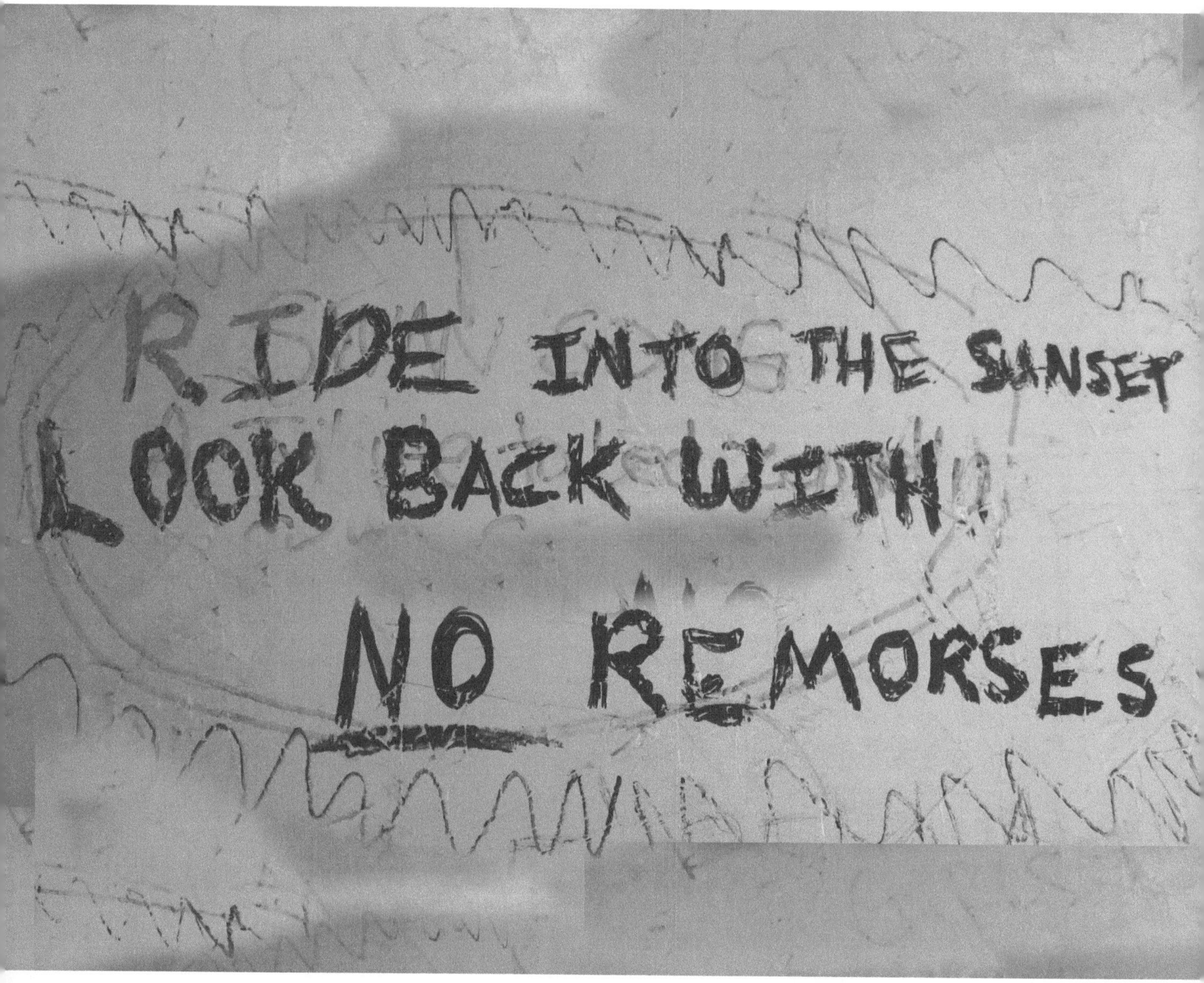

RIDE INTO THE SUNSET
LOOK BACK WITH
NO REMORSES

This Book is dedicated
to all the unknown
Artist and Philosophers

When I began this project a few years ago, I never really thought about how temporary these little gems I would find really were. Most came from a bar I frequent. The Vagina one, which is wildly popular, came from a bar in Austin. When I went back a year later, it had been crossed out, so I placed one of the stickers I had made underneath where it once was. Most of what is in this book has since been crossed out, drawn on, or painted over... I now know this project needs to continue...These hilarious (and sometimes too deep to be on a restroom wall) words need to be captured.

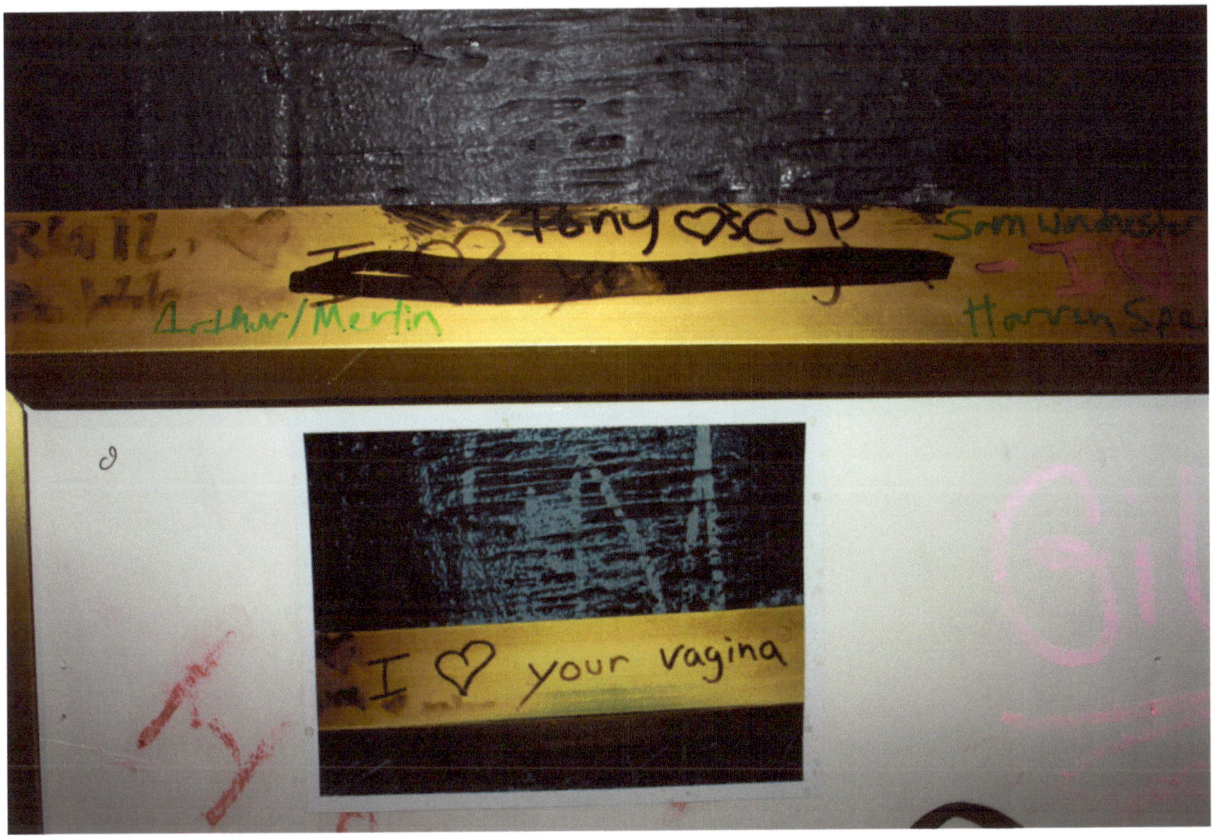

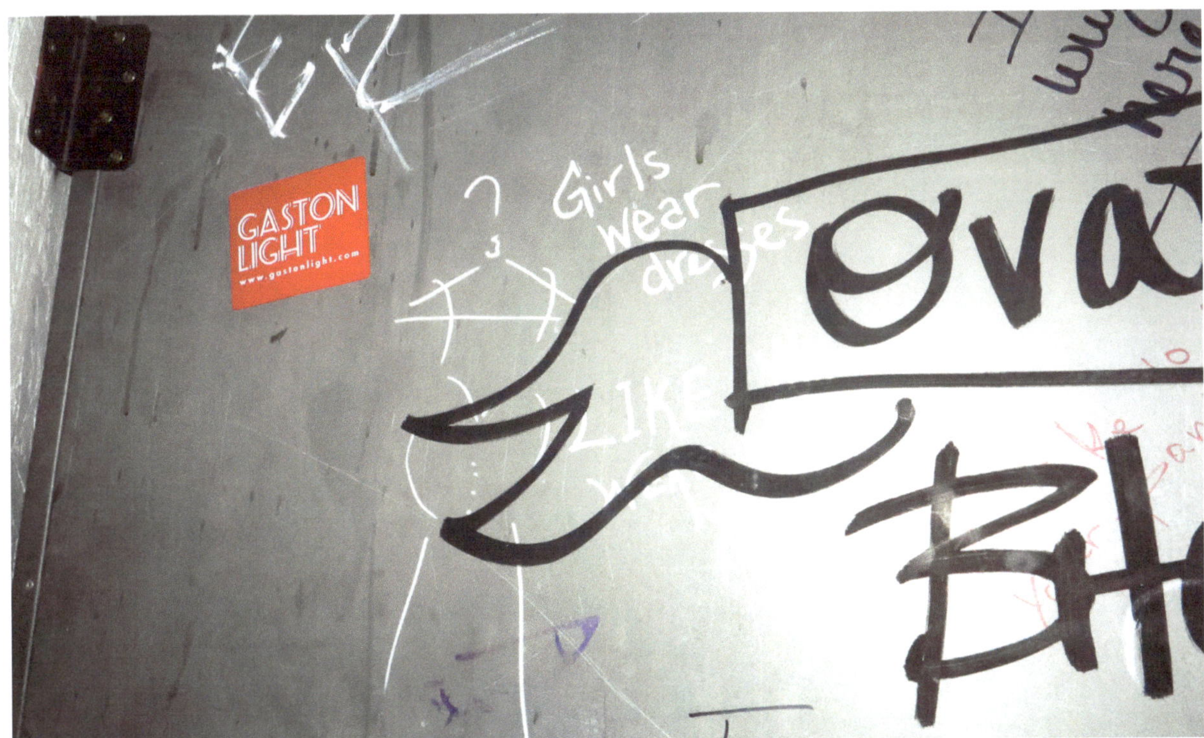
GASTON LIGHT
www.gastonlight.com
?
Girls wear dresses
LIKE
Ova
BH
ER

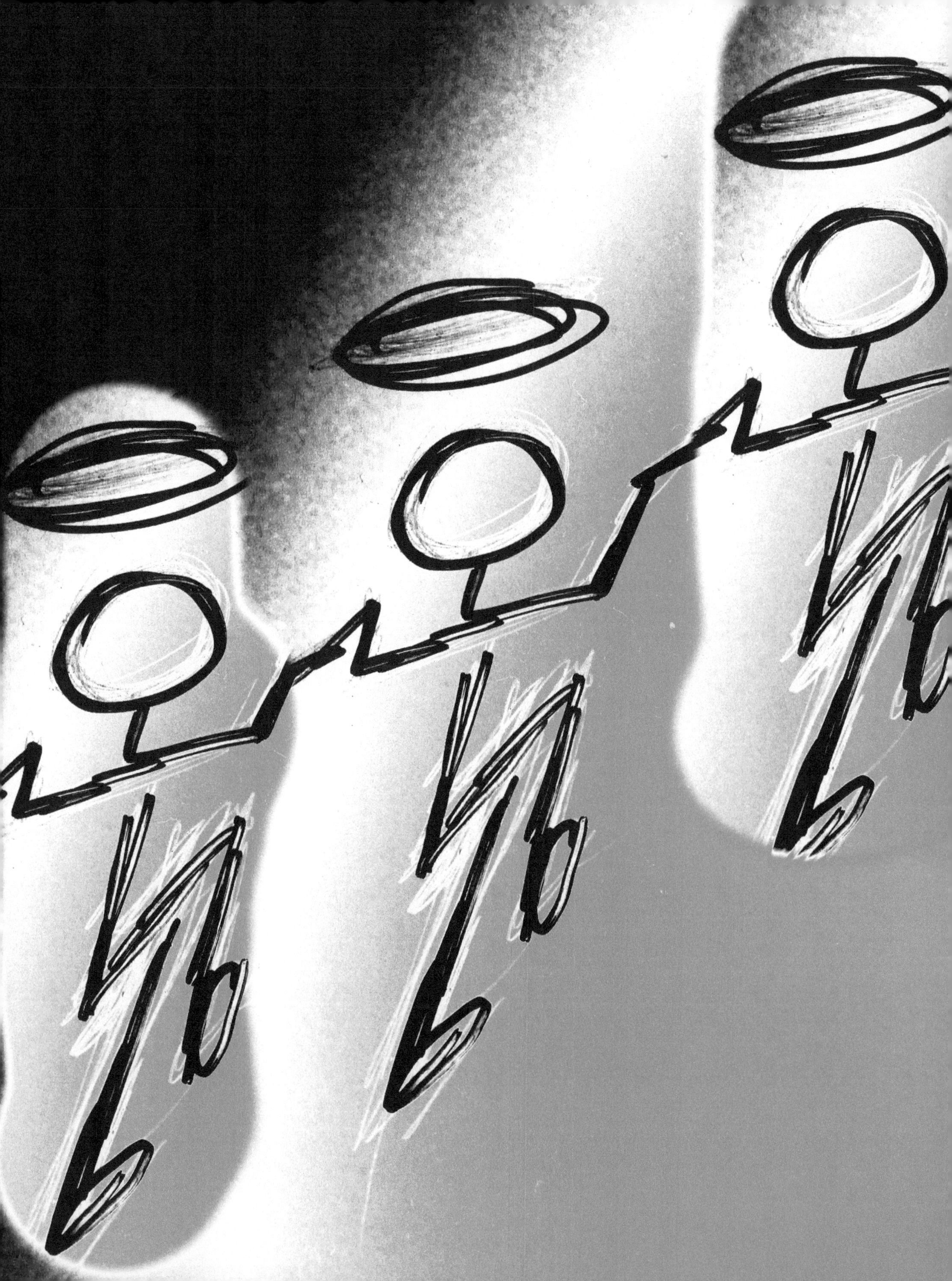

It's the Devil I Love

666

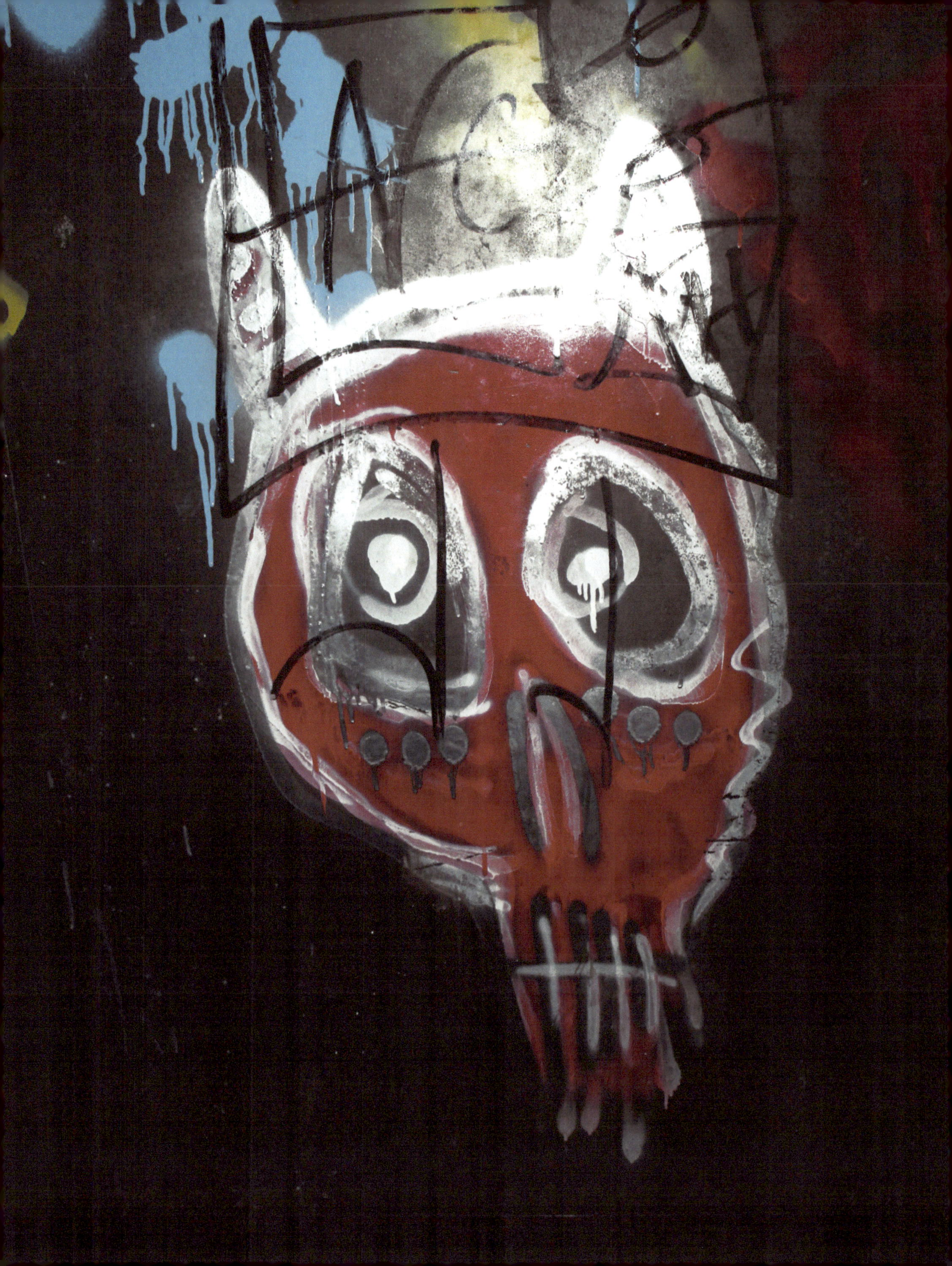

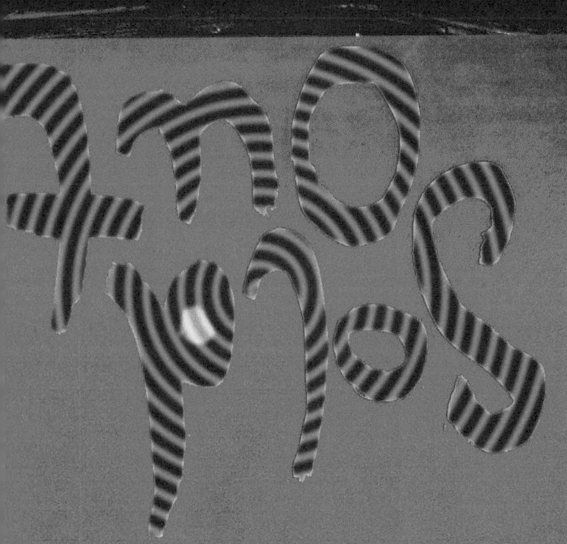

sold
out

you and me

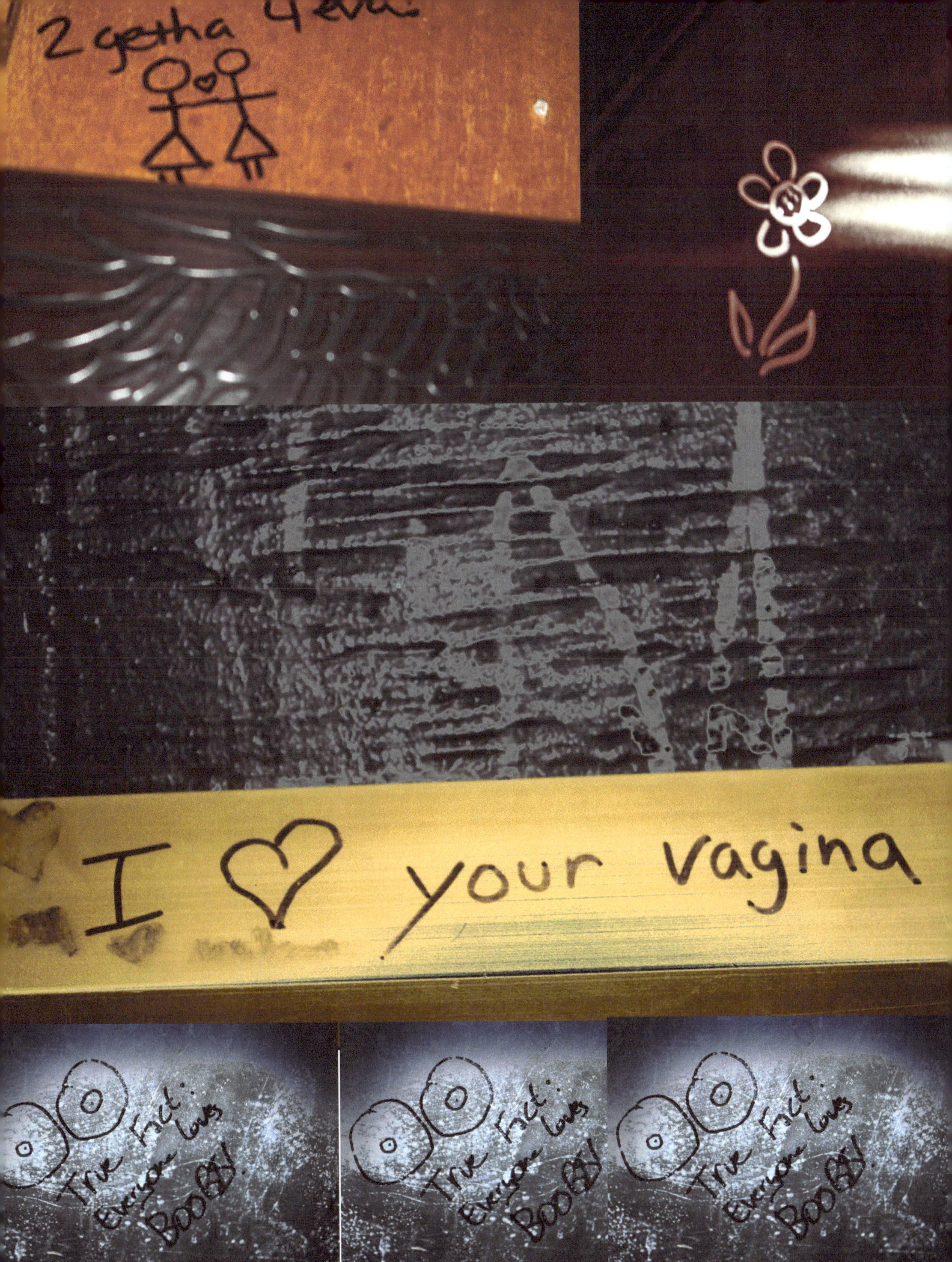

2getha 4eva
I ♥ your vagina
True Fact: Everyone loves BOOBS!
True Fact: Everyone loves BOOBS!
True Fact: Everyone loves BOOBS!

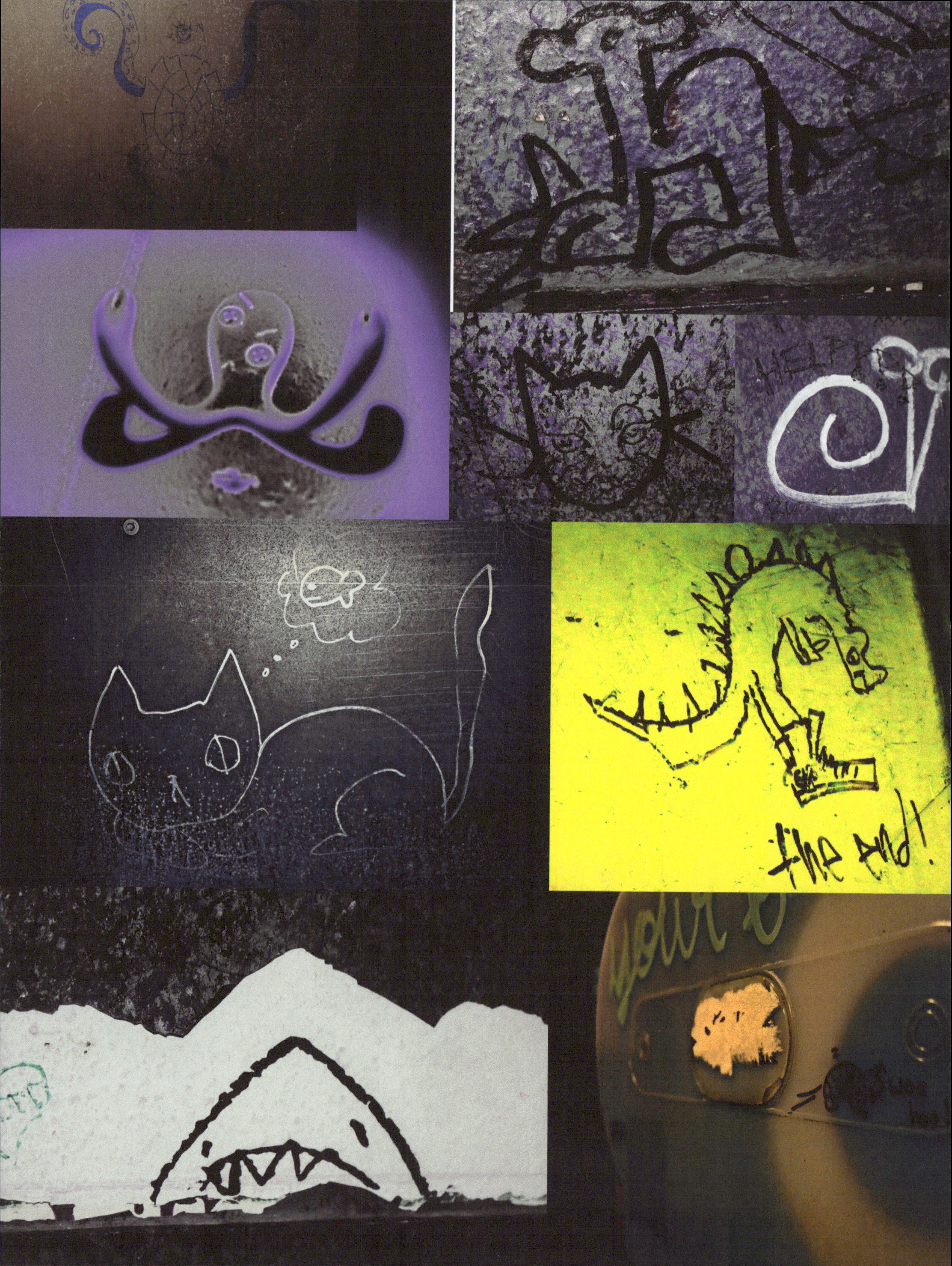
HELP
the end!
your

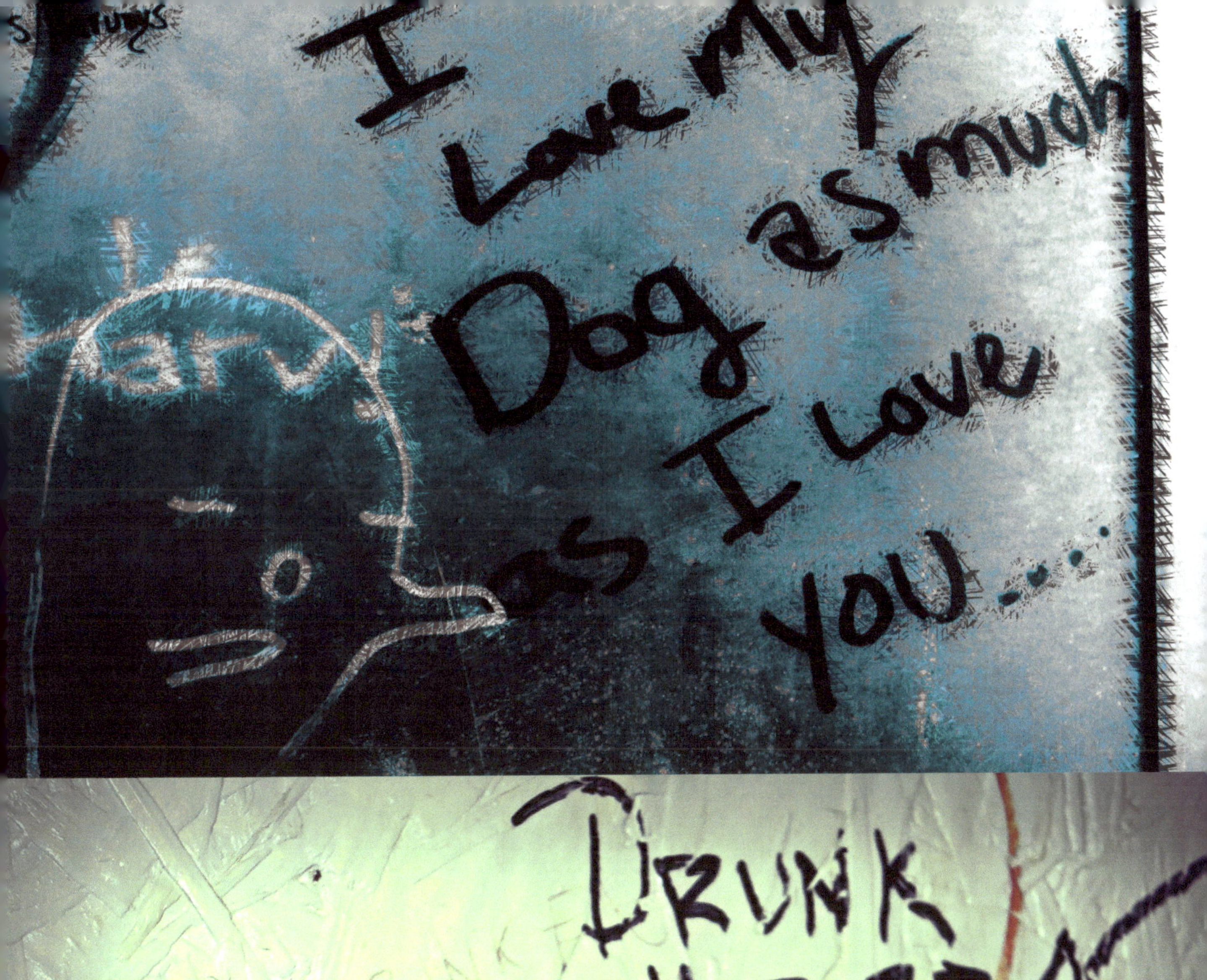

I Love my Dog as much as I love you.....
Drunk Hitler Octopus wants to fight you!
This serves No purpose.

Live
Laugh
Love

Girls wear dresses LIKE YOU WEAR YOUR SHAM[E]

I LIKE BIG BUTTS AND I CANNOT LIE

I got married... WTF?
I got married... WTF?

why??

why??   I got married... why??

got married... WTF?

got married... WTF?   why??

The caffine
made me do it--

The caffine
made me do it--

You left your
panties @ my
mom
go hom

house !!! ...
those r notmypanties
!!! ...you're drunk
- DAD

Look at
yourself
you are a
fucking
Beautiful
Creation

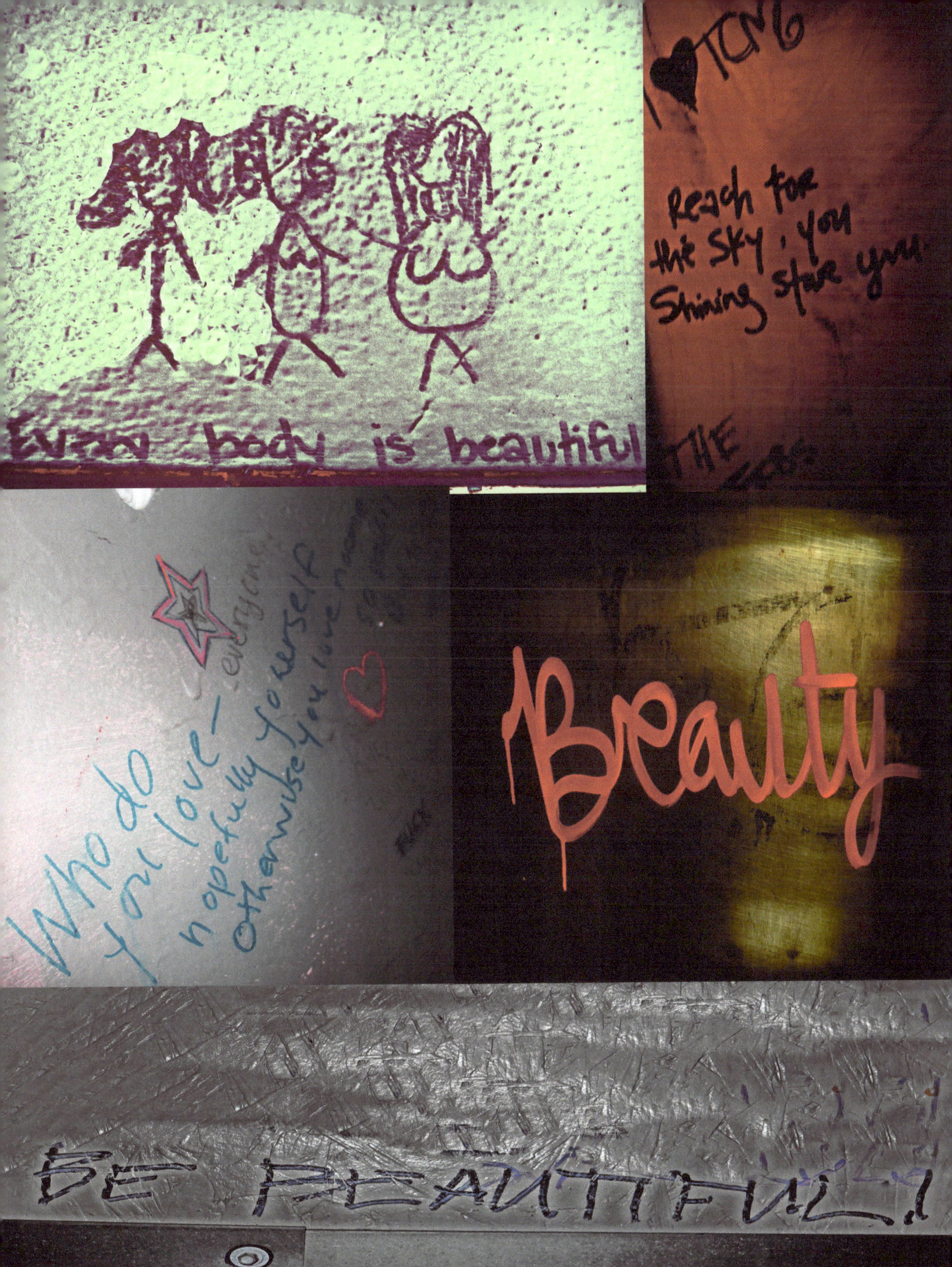
Every body is beautiful
I ♥ TCM6
Reach for the sky, you shining star you
THE
Who do you love — everyone, hopefully. Otherwise love yourself
Beauty
BE BEAUTIFUL..!

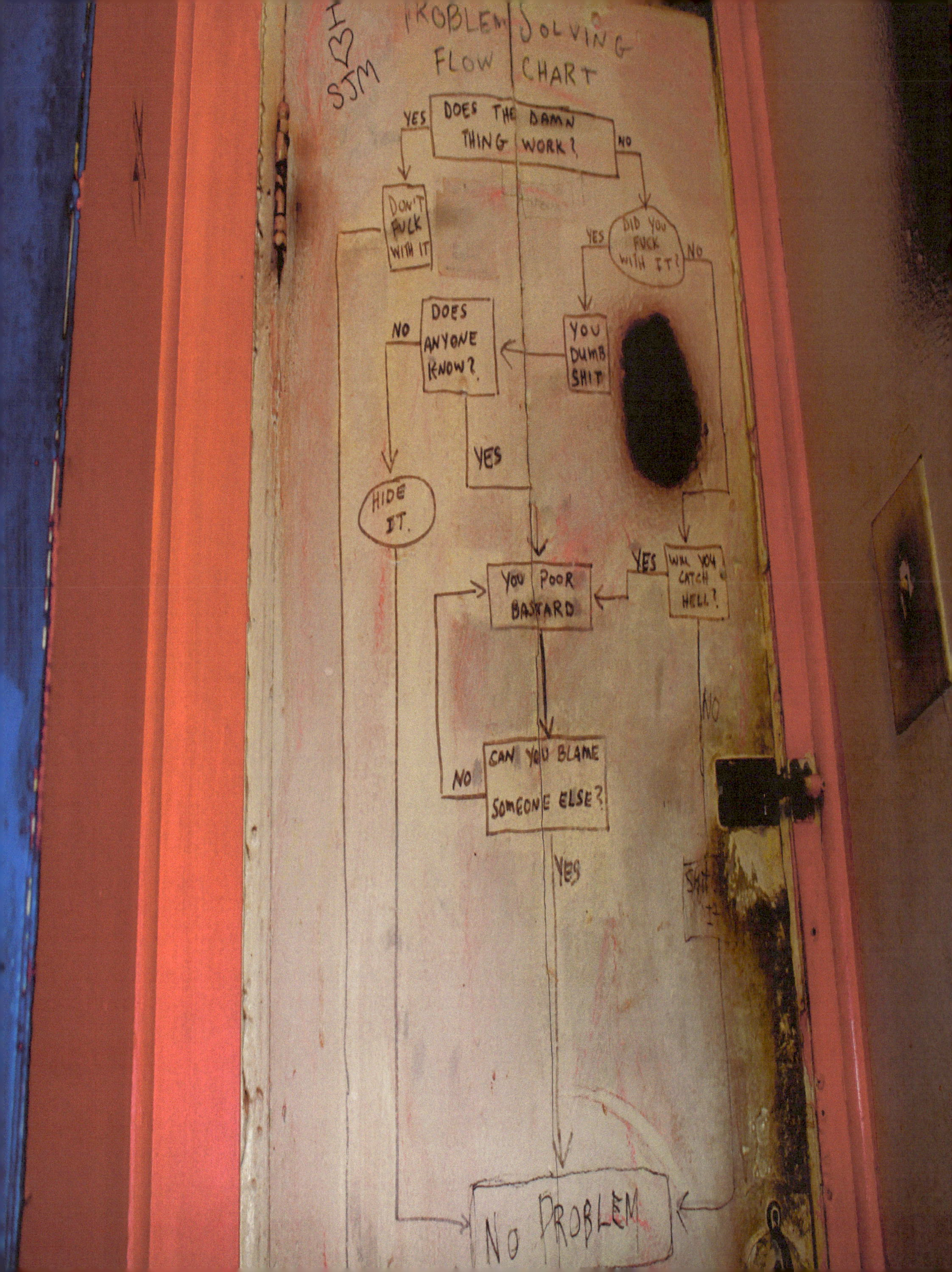
SJM
PROBLEM SOLVING
FLOW CHART
DOES THE DAMN THING WORK?
YES
NO
DON'T FUCK WITH IT
DID YOU FUCK WITH IT?
YES
NO
DOES ANYONE KNOW?
NO
YOU DUMB SHIT
YES
HIDE IT.
YOU POOR BASTARD
YES
WILL YOU CATCH HELL?
YES
NO
CAN YOU BLAME SOMEONE ELSE?
NO
YES
SHIT
NO PROBLEM

SOMEONE CALL HEALTH SERVICES!!! ASAP!!!

good tunes
good brew
good buddies

look out
for rain
IPEE
WITH
SHARPIES

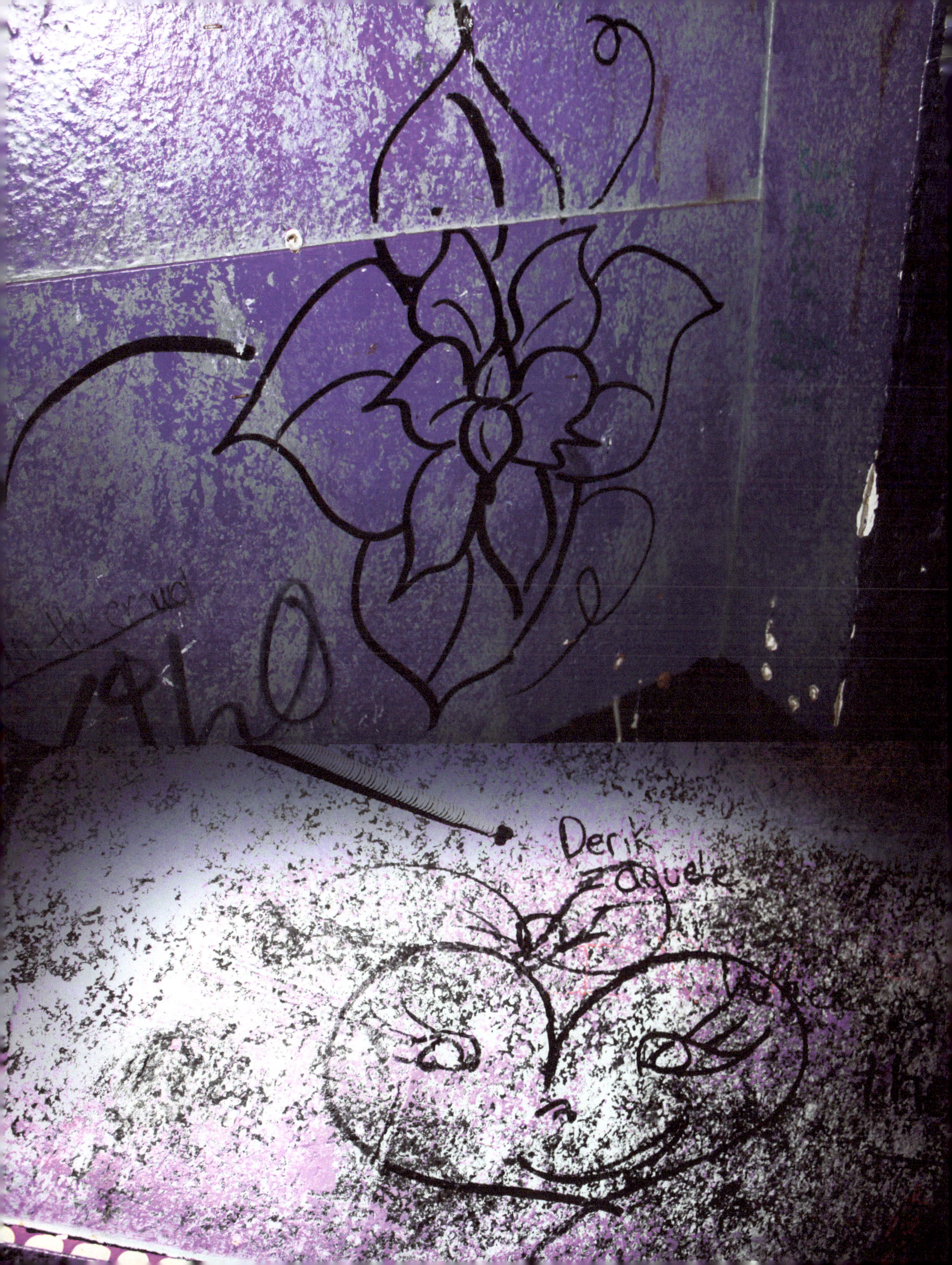
Derik
Zadvele

Beware the
deathly
Hallows

EMBRACE THE STRUGGLE

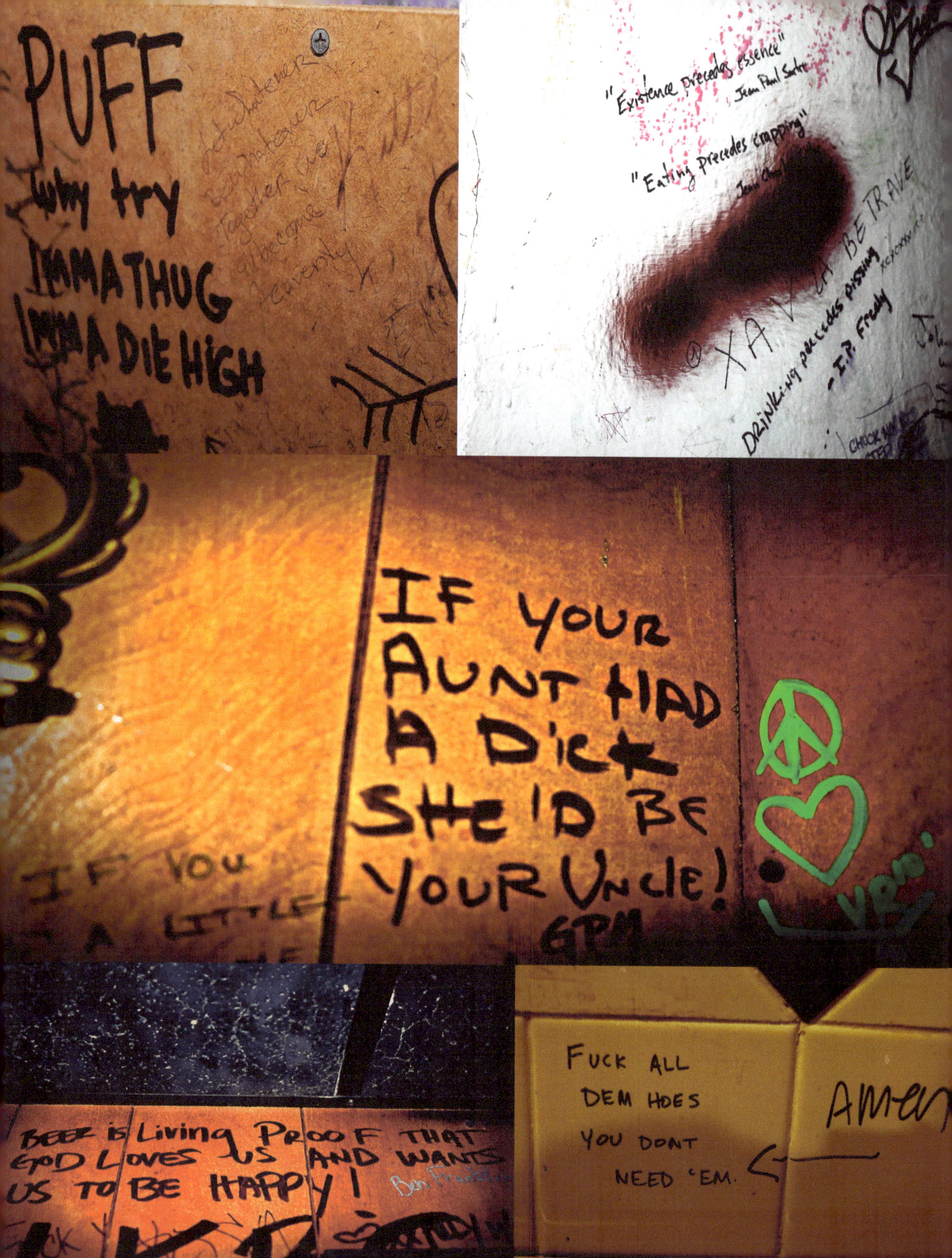
PUFF
why try
IMMA THUG
IMMA DIE HIGH

"Existence precedes essence"
Jean Paul Sartre
"Eating precedes crapping"
Jean Cho
Drinking precedes pissing
- I.P. Freely
BE TRAVE

IF YOUR
AUNT HAD
A DICK
SHE'D BE
YOUR UNCLE!
6PM
IF YOU
A LITTLE

BEER IS LIVING PROOF THAT
GOD LOVES US AND WANTS
US TO BE HAPPY!
Ben Franklin

FUCK ALL
DEM HOES
YOU DONT
NEED 'EM.
Amen

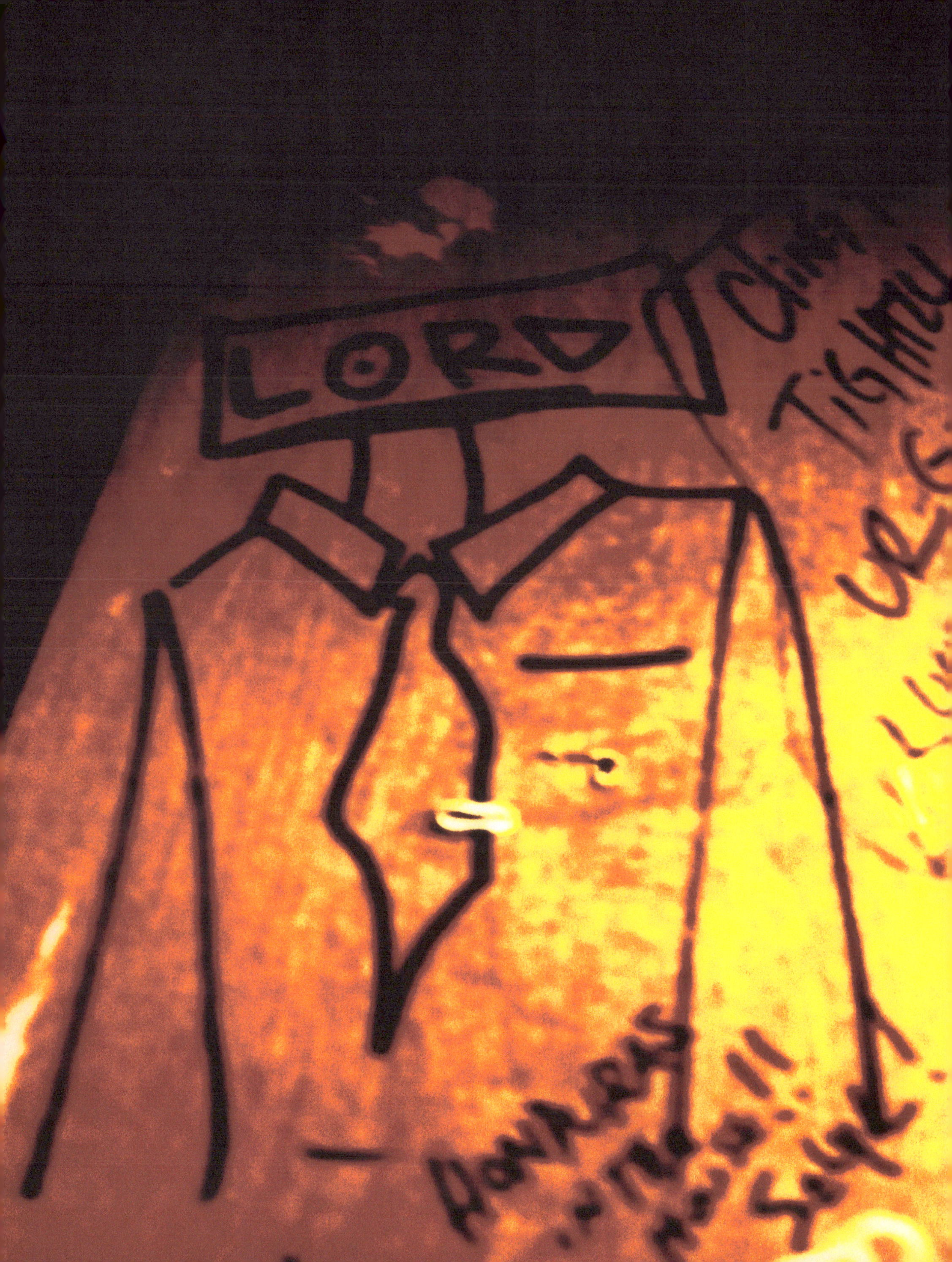
LORD

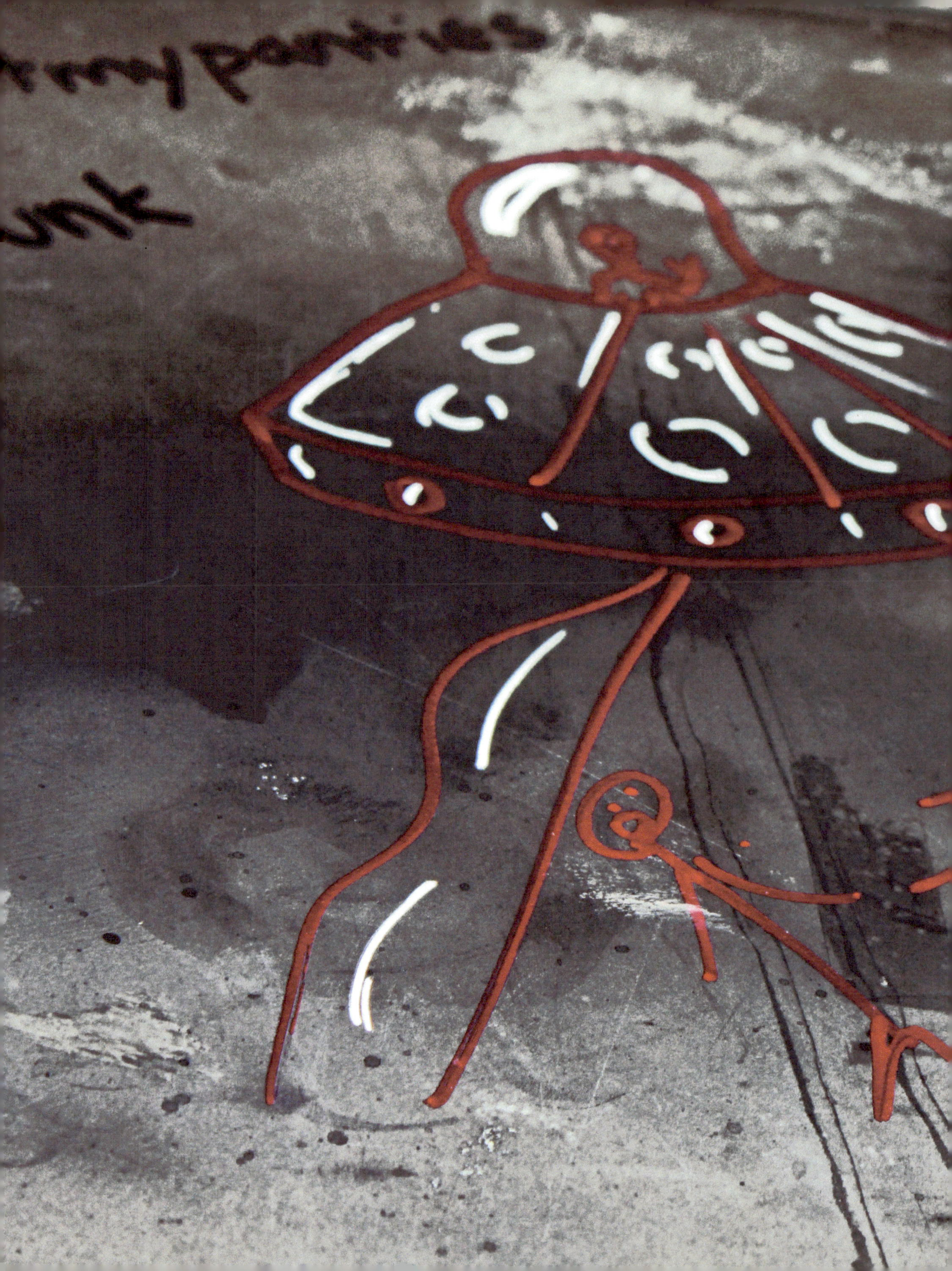

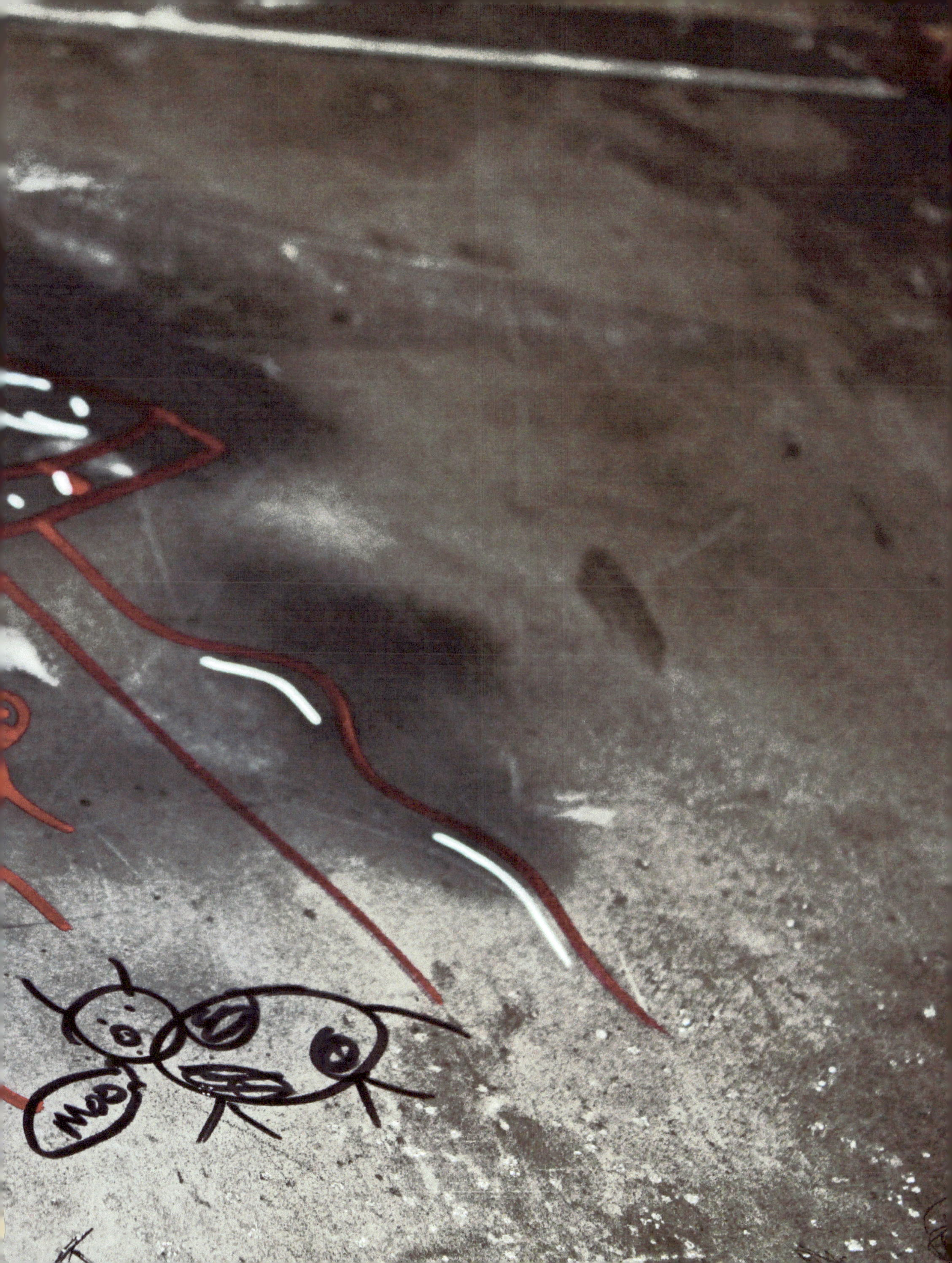

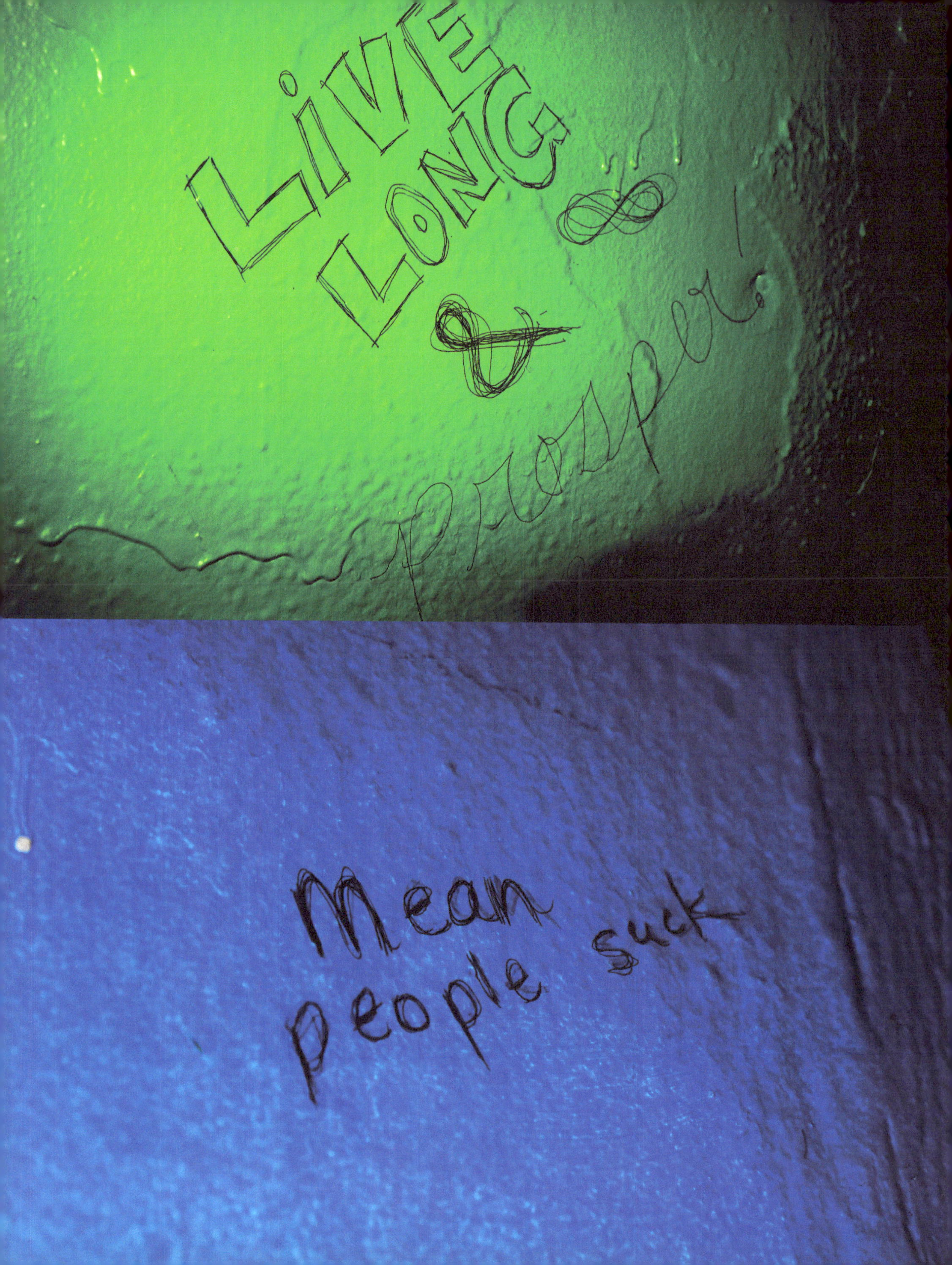

LIVE LONG & prosper
Mean people suck

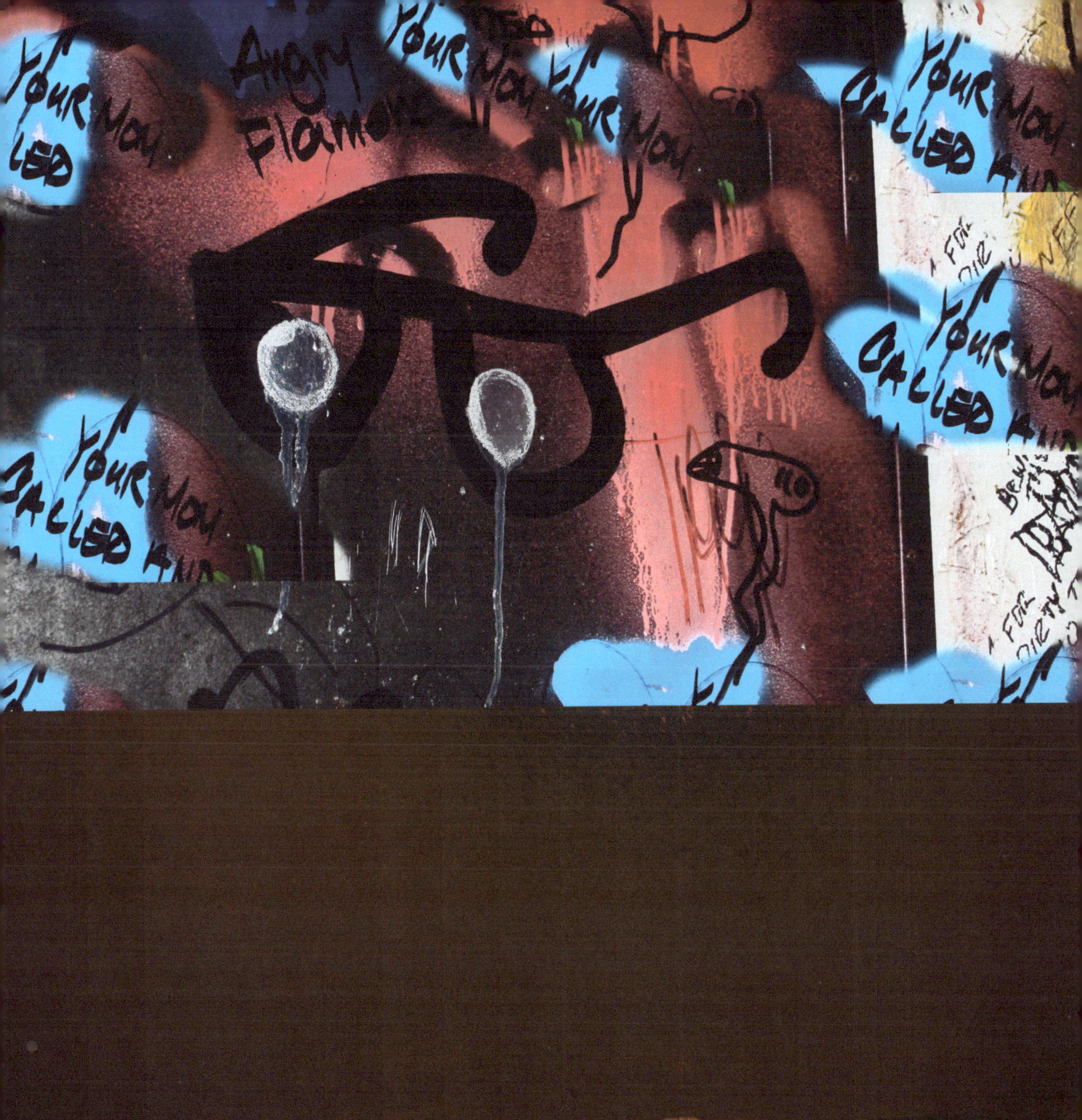
Your Mom
LED
Angry
Flamonde
Your Mom
Your Mom
Your Mom
CALLED AND
Your Mom
CALLED AND
Your Mom
CALLED AND
your face

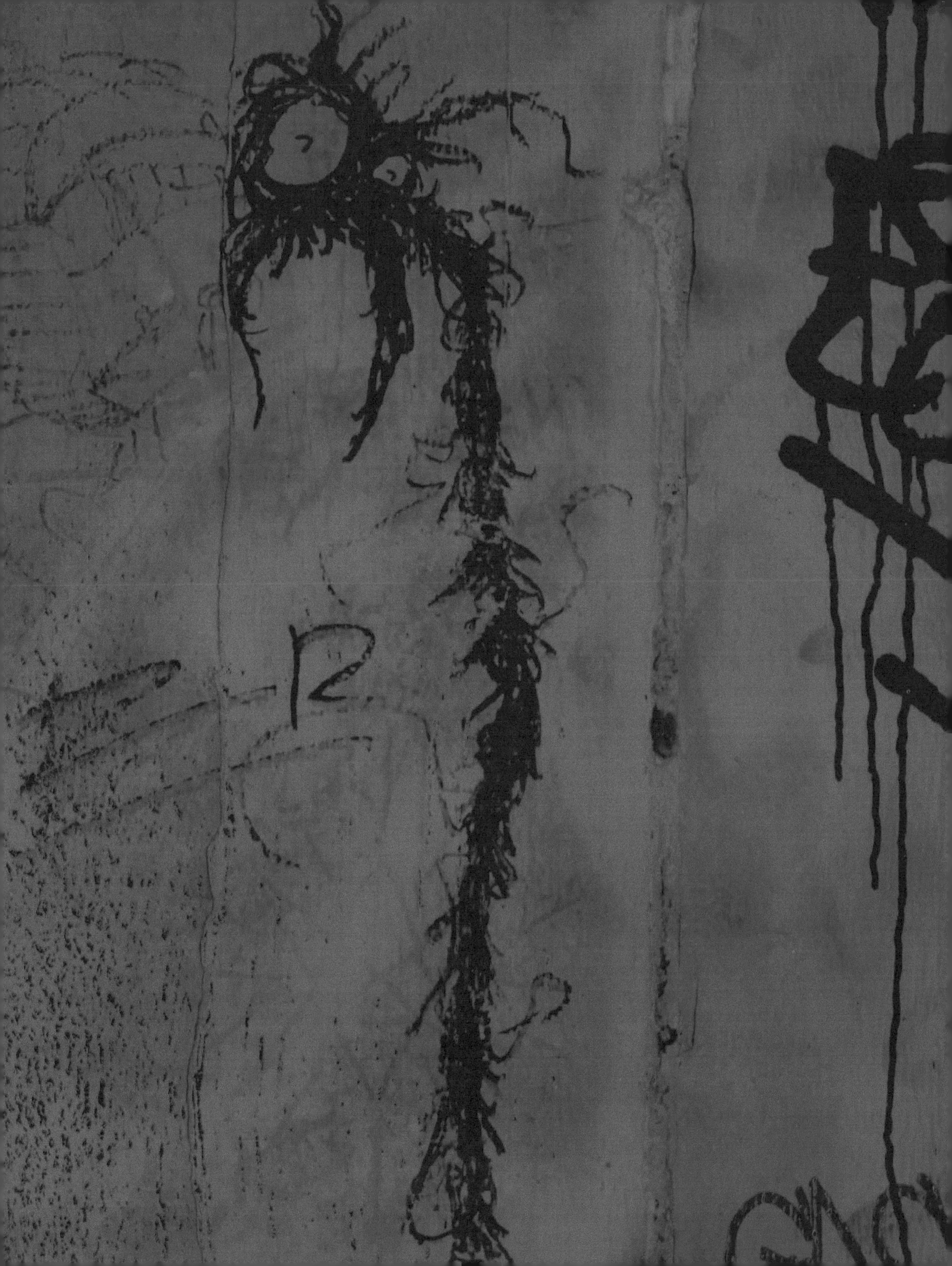

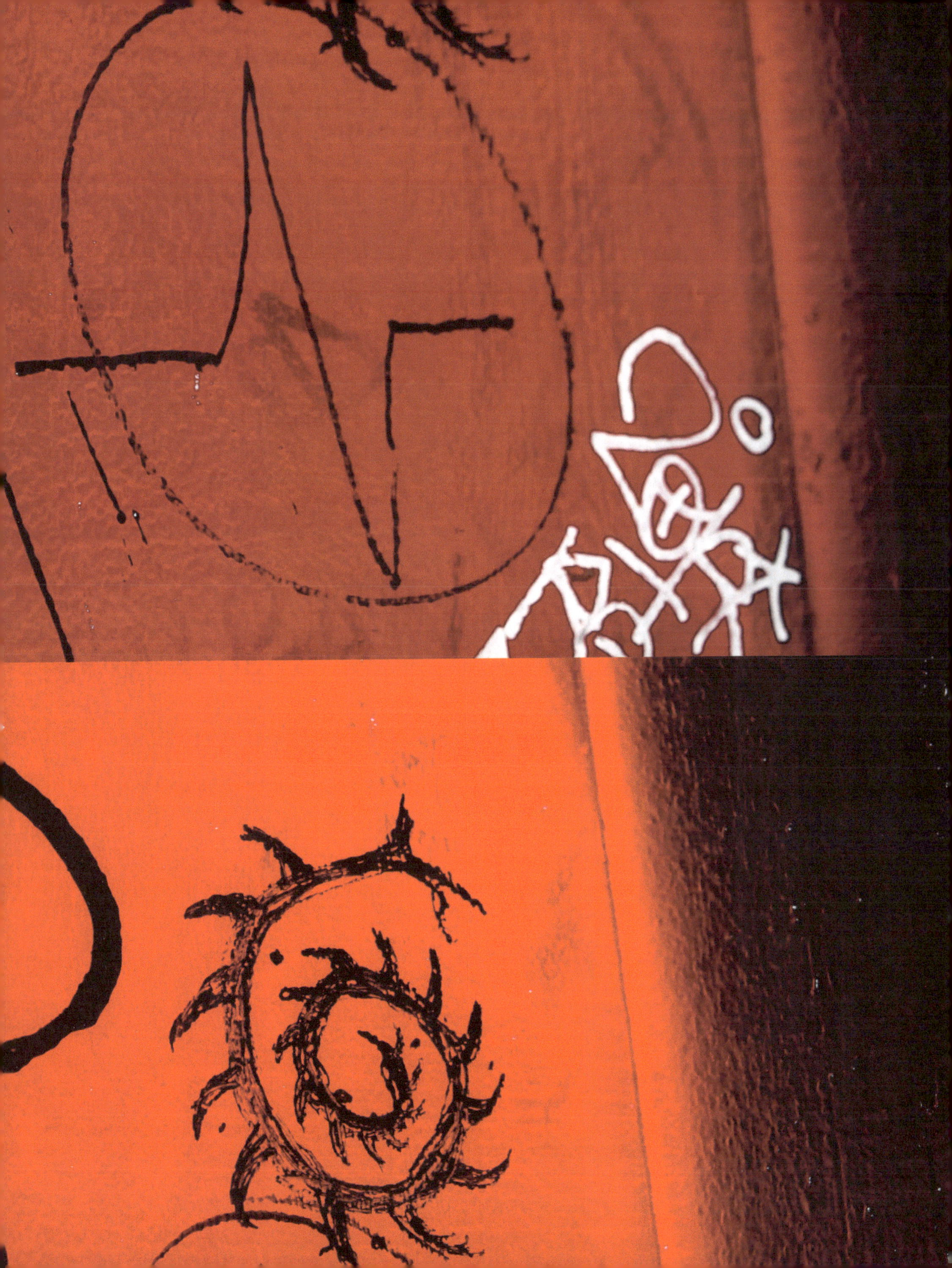

stand You!

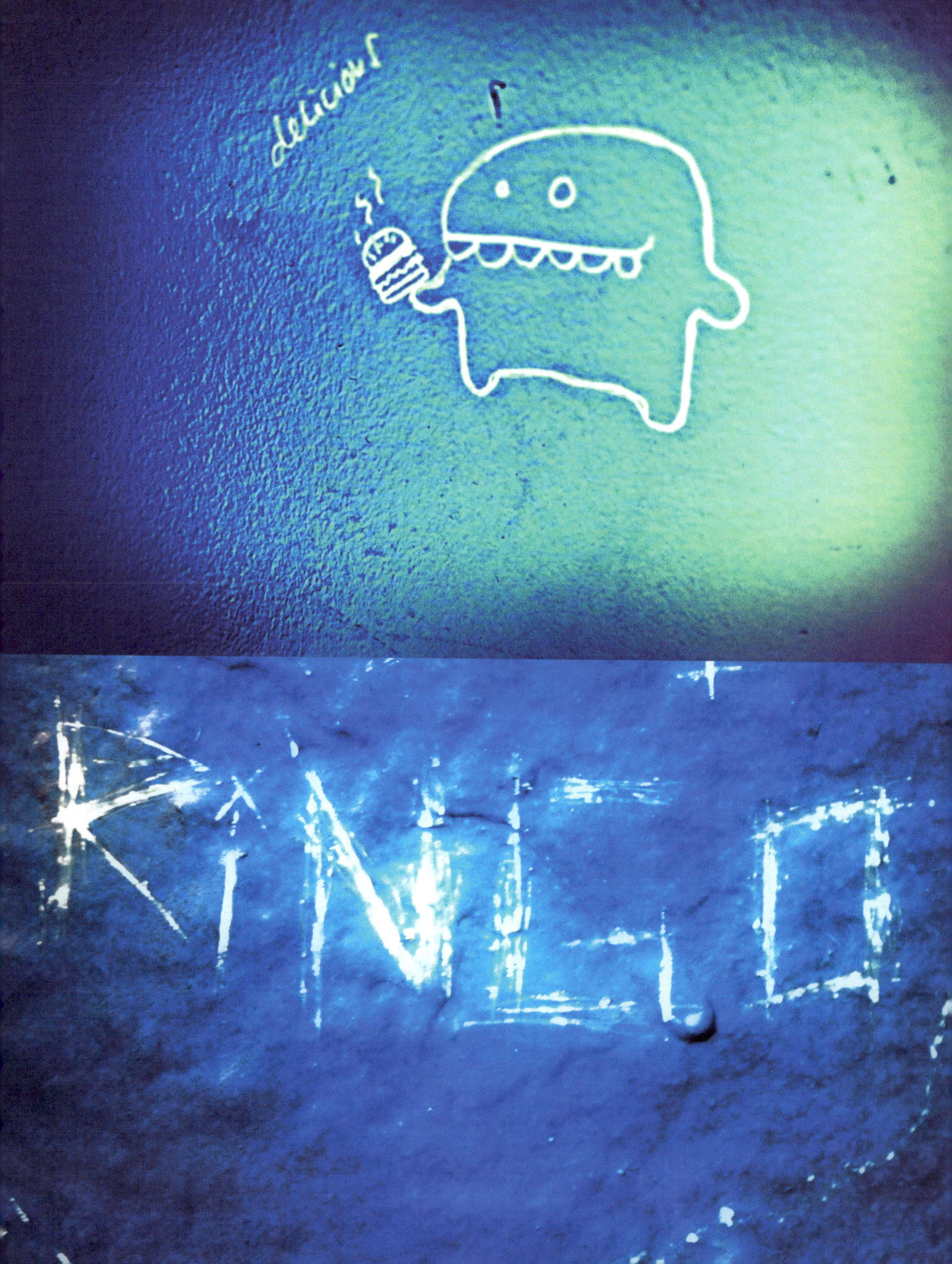

delicious

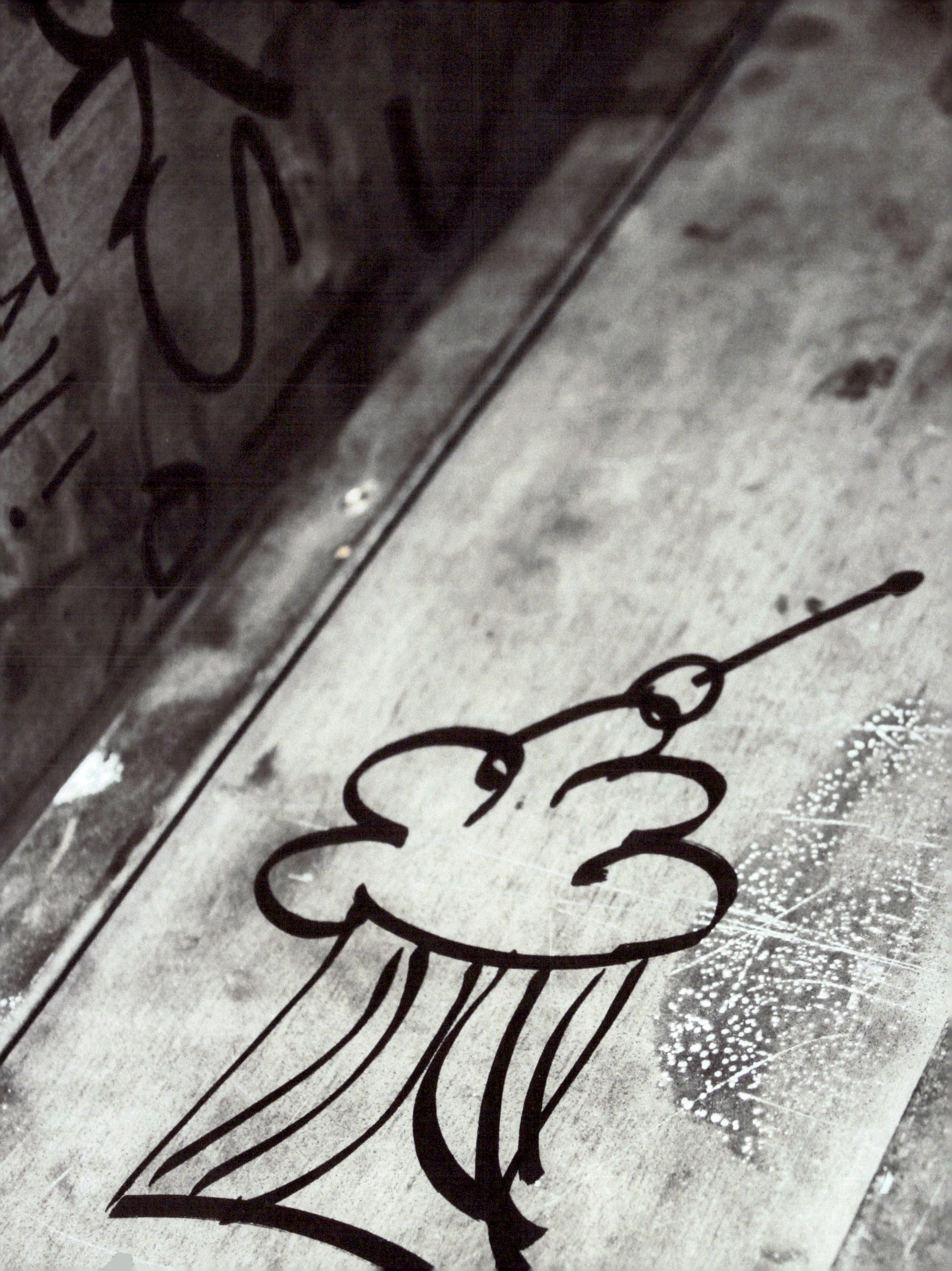

for a good
call
800-

me
suck-it

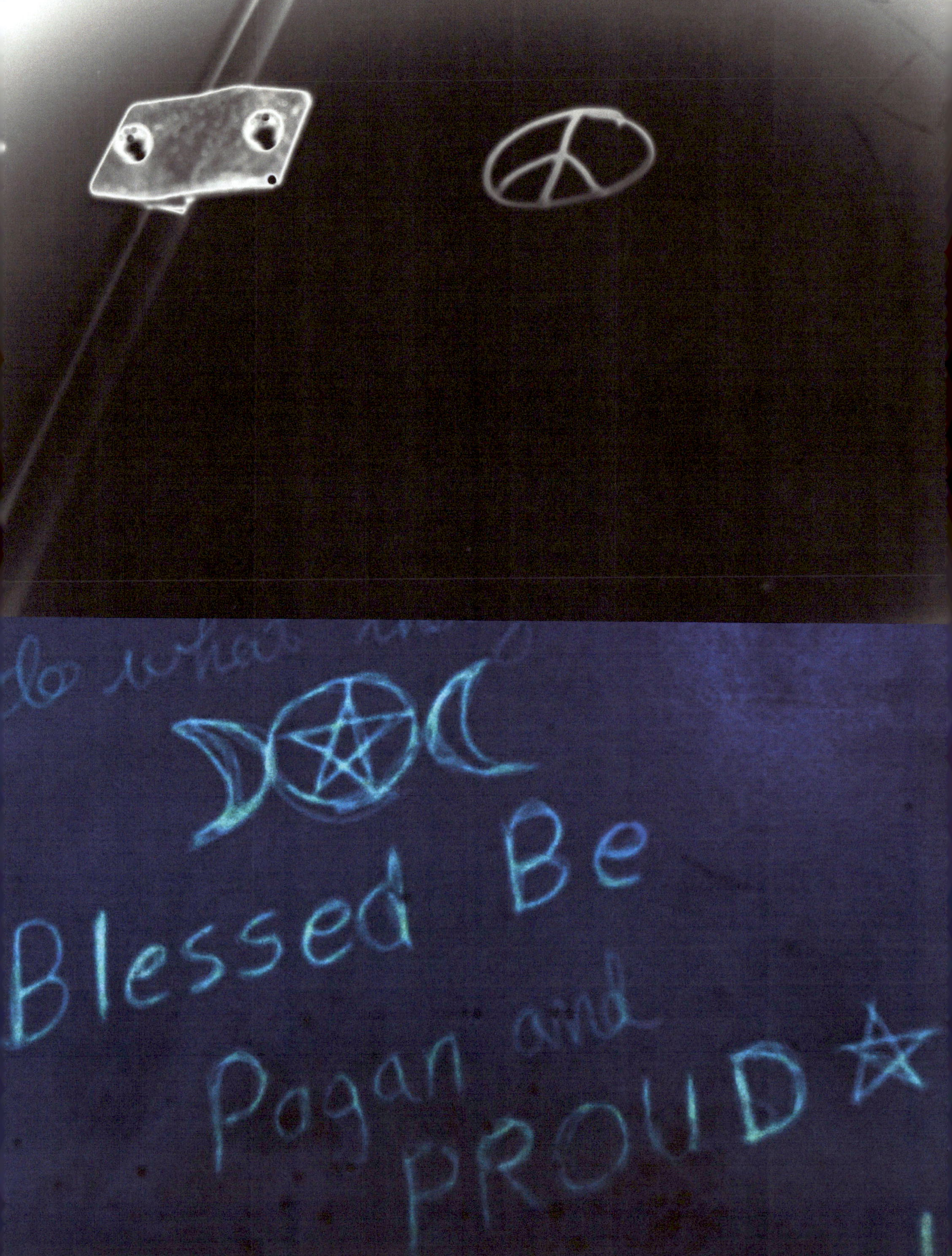
Blessed Be
Pagan and
PROUD ☆

I ♥

~~YUPPIES~~
~~PUNKS~~
~~RAVERS~~
~~GOTHS~~
~~EMO BOYS~~
IPSTERS

* WITH ART
DEGREES
THAT WORK @
STARBUXS...

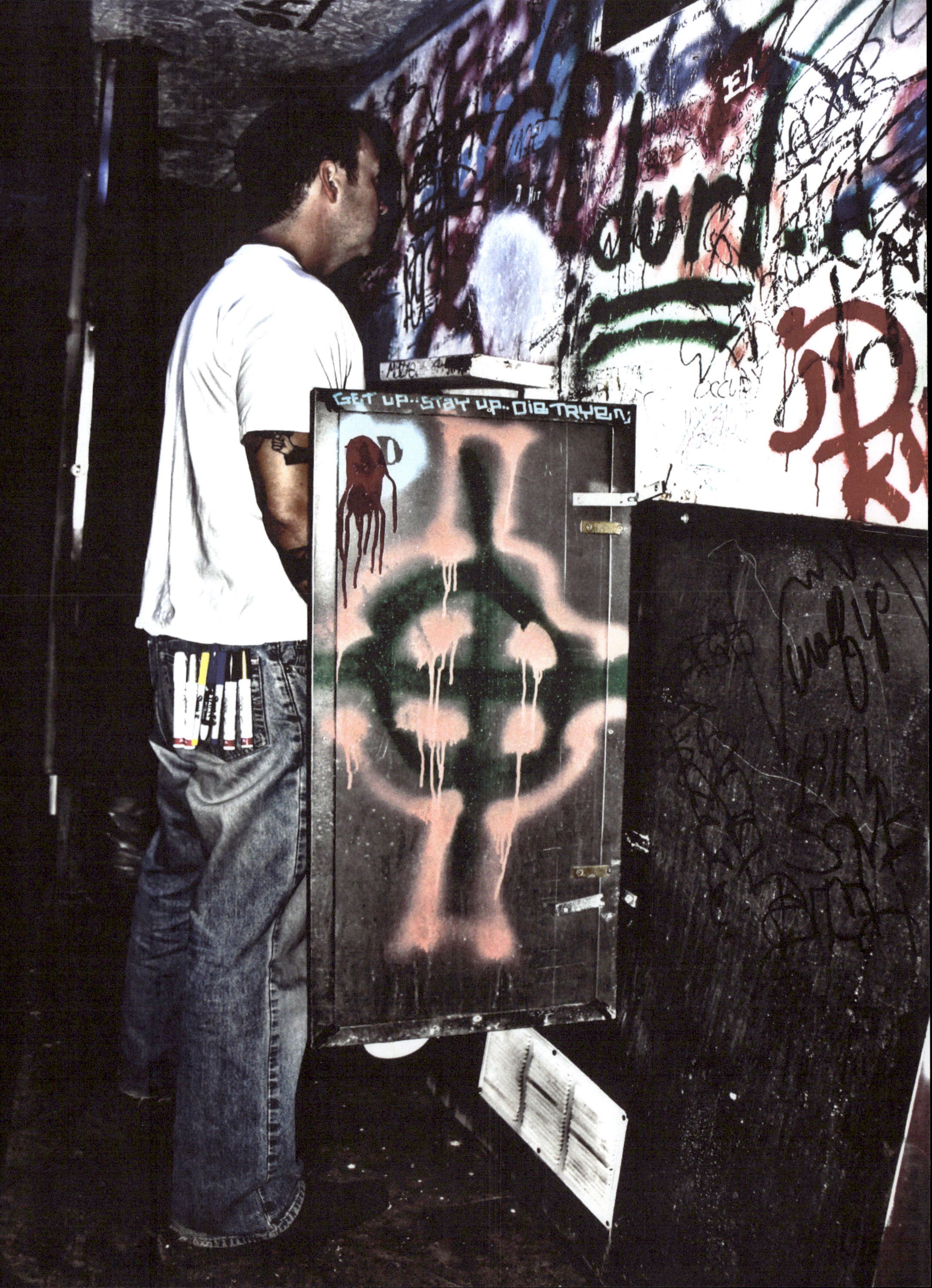

GET UP..STAY UP..DIE TRYEN

A very Special Thank You to

Trigger Mortis & Scott Lewis
for being my cover models.

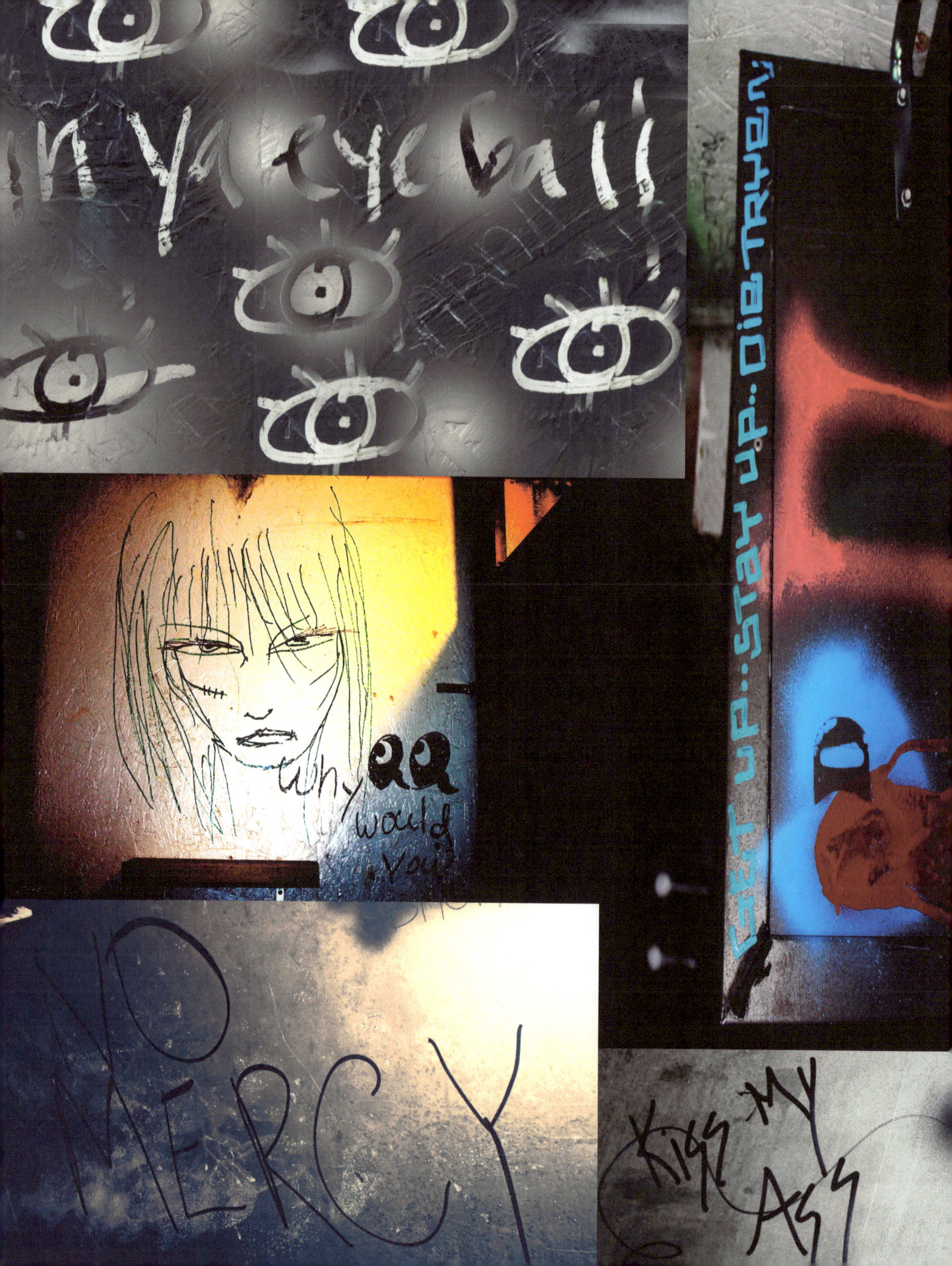
n ya eye ball
why
would you?
GET UP.. STAY UP.. DIE TRYEN.
NO
MERCY
KISS MY
ASS

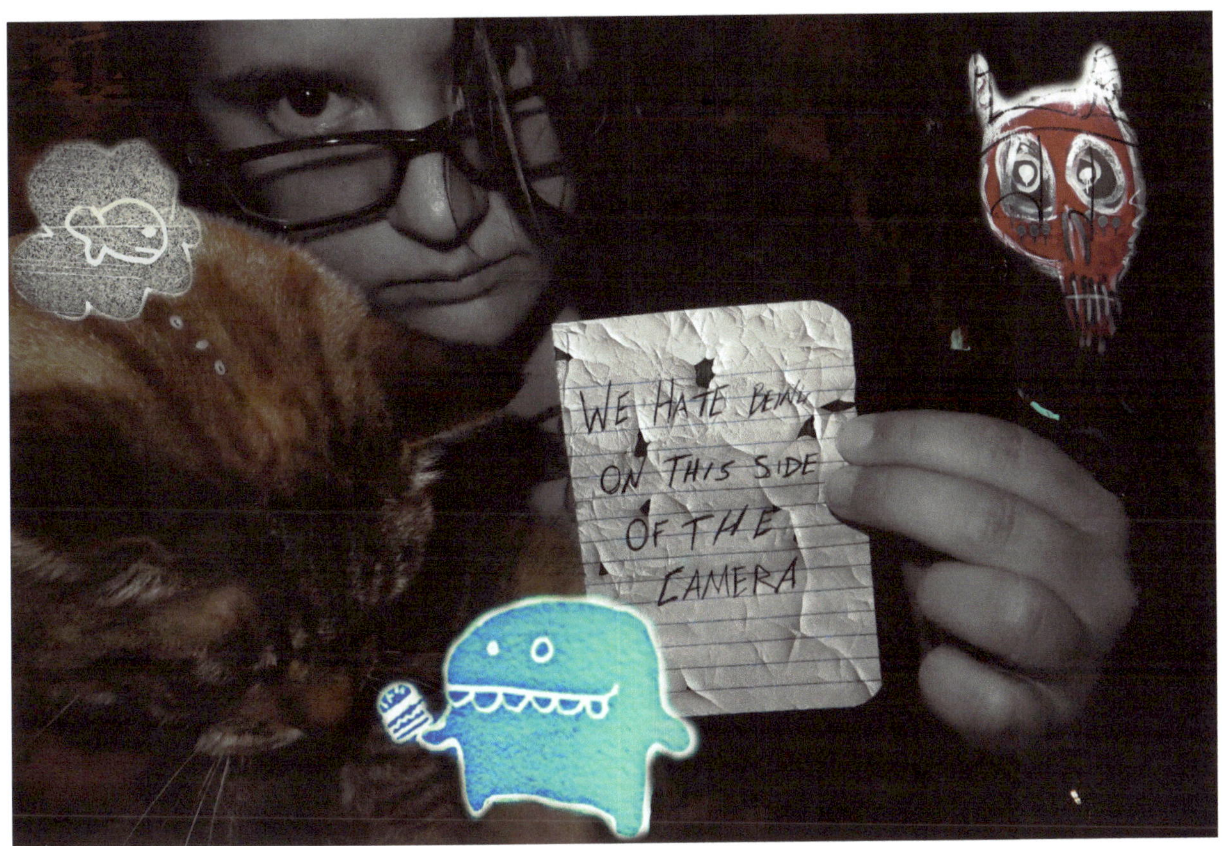

Ashley, who prefers to be called Ash, and introduces herself as such (though everyone always repeats back "Ashley") is a Dallas based photographer and writer. She started photographing things at the age of four and never stopped. Once she was older and discovered programs like Photoshop her imagination went on a rampage. She began writing poetry and journaling in grade school and continues to this day. She has an eye for turning things into artwork that were never meant to be art. She lives for bad jokes, puns, and word play. She thrives on the mockery of social norms and carries with her a morbid sense of humor and outlook on life.

Contact: Ash.Poetic.Photographer@live.com